BUDDHIS
BEGINNER

The Top Secret Buddhism Guide for Living a Balanced Life

TABLE OF CONTENTS

Copyright Notice

Disclaimer

While all attempts have been made to verify the information provided in this book, the author does not assume any responsibility for errors, omissions, or contrary interpretations of the subject matter contained within. The information provided in this book is for educational and entertainment purposes only. The reader is responsible for his or her own actions and the author does not accept any responsibilities for any liabilities or damages, real or perceived, resulting from the use of this information.

INTRODUCTION

Here is a place where you can learn about the secrets in the ways that Buddhists live their lives, and how Buddhism challenges modern life.

In addition to a bit of history about the religion, including the first Buddha, we'll show you the important doctrines and teaching of Buddhism, in a way that is easy to follow and understand.

This book is filled with wisdom and common sense that will help you to understand all the facets of life in Buddhism.

You will learn about:

- The first Buddha

- Different schools of Buddhism

- How to understand and utilize meditation

- What Buddhism means in everyday life

- Letting go of suffering and embracing joy

- Finding your own spiritual path

You can use this book right now to learn more about this popular idea – the work of transcending the mundane aspects of your life and discovering your own true path to happiness. Once you know Buddhism well, you will understand why it helps so many people in this troubled world to find peace and enlightenment within themselves.

CHAPTER 1 – What is Buddhism all about?

Buddha Shakyamuni founded Buddhism and he lived and taught people about 2,500 years ago. Since that time, millions of people all over the world have followed the path of pure spirituality that he taught. The way of life for a Buddhist is one of wisdom, peace and loving kindness. It is absolutely as relevant for people today as it was in the ancient days in India.

Buddha explained to followers that our earthly suffering and problems come from negative and confused states of mind, while all of our good fortune and happiness come from positive and peaceful mind states.

He taught people methods to overcome their negative minds, and the teachings are still helpful today. You can learn to overcome your negative mind states, like ignorance, anger and jealousy, and develop your positive mind with wisdom, love and compassion. Only through these steps will you be able to experience true happiness and lasting peace.

These positive methods can still work for any person, of any age, in any part of the world. Once you gain the experience yourself, you can pass it on to other people, so that they can enjoy the positive benefits, as well.

The Spiritual Path

Buddha's teachings reveal a simple path that will lead you to lasting happiness. When you follow this path, you can transform your mind gradually from a self-centered, confused state into Buddhism's blissful mind.

Meditation

The heart of the way of life for Buddhists is meditation. This is a way to work on and understand your own mind. You will first learn to identify your various negative mental states (these are called "delusions") and then to develop positive and peaceful mental states (known as "virtuous minds").

In meditation, Buddhists overcome their delusions by becoming more familiar with the habits of virtuous minds. Through meditation, you can maintain a virtuous mind and use your wisdom to solve the many problems we all face today. As your mind becomes more positive, then your actions will become constructive, and your life experience will become more satisfying to you and more beneficial for others.

Almost anyone is capable of learning the basic techniques of meditation to experience its benefits, but progressing beyond simple meditation requires you to have faith in the Three Buddhist Jewels, who are Buddha, Sangha and Dharma. This usually develops in a natural way, as you experience the benefits of your meditation.

Can anyone become a Buddha?

Geshe Kelsang states that every living person has within themselves the potential to truly become a Buddha. This means someone who has purified his mind of limitations and faults, and has perfected his good qualities. Your mind is like the sky on a cloudy day – it is pure and clear, but overcast by delusion's clouds.

Just as even the heaviest storm clouds disperse eventually, in the same way your heaviest delusions can be removed from your mind. Delusions like ignorance, hatred and greed are not intrinsic aspects of your mind. If you use the proper methods, you can eliminate them completely and experience full enlightenment and happiness.

After you attain enlightenment, you will have all the qualities you need to bring other living beings into the same state of exaltedness. These qualities are boundless spiritual power, omniscient wisdom, compassion and universal love. This is the ultimate goal of Mahayana Buddhism.

The History of Buddhism

Buddha Shakyamuni was born in 624 BC as a royal prince in Lumbini. At one time the village was in northern India, but it is now in the country of Nepal. The name of his royal family is Shakya and the "Muni" in his name means an "able one".

His parents called him Siddhartha, and many positive predictions were made about what his future would hold. He lived in a royal palace in his youth, but left at age 29 and retired to the forested land in the country. There he spent his time in meditation in a spiritual life. He attained his enlightenment after just six years in Bodh Gaya, India, under the Bodhi Tree.

Buddha was requested to teach the people, and he rose from his meditation to teach the First Wheel of Dharma. The teachings in this wheel include the Sutra of Four Noble truths, along with other discourses which form the principal source of Hinayana, which is the lesser vehicle of the Buddhist religion.

Later, Buddha would teach both second and third Wheels of Dharma, including the Sutra of Perfection of Wisdom and the

Sutra Discriminating the Intention. These important teachings are the source of the Great Vehicle, or Mahayana, of Buddhism.

Buddha explains in the Hinayana teachings how you can attain liberation from your suffering. He explains the means of attaining full enlightening, known as Buddhahood, for other people's sake. Both of these traditions have flourished in India and then elsewhere in Asia, and spread to Tibet and other neighboring countries. They are beginning also to flourish in the Western world.

Buddha Shakyamuni taught 84,000 teachings in all. His intent was founding Buddhism to lead all living things to a permanent release from their suffering. He understood that liberation from difficulties and suffering as a temporary thing was not enough. His goal was helping living people to find Nirvana, or lasting peace, and he was motivated by compassion and love to make it so.

CHAPTER 2 – What do Buddhists believe?

When you are a beginner in Buddhism, you will receive doctrine lists. They are known as:

- The Eightfold Path

- The Five Skandhas

- The Four Noble Truths

You will be instructed to learn the teachings of Buddha, and to practice them in your own life. However, believing in Buddhism's doctrines is not the real point of Buddhism.

The only historical Buddha taught a method to help you understand yourself and the world in a different way. You are not meant to accept the many doctrines lists on blind faith. You should not be bound to – or idolatrous about – any ideology, doctrine or theory, not even Buddhism's. The systems of thought for Buddhist's are a way to guide you, rather than an absolute truth.

Thich Nhat Hanh speaks of absolute truth, but this can't be contained in concepts or words, as you know them. Believing merely in the concepts and words is not the path for a Buddhist to take. As an example, believing in reincarnation or rebirth have no point if you only believe in the statements. You must, rather, practice Buddhism, so that you can realize a self that isn't subject to earthly birth and death.

Many Boats, only One River

Even though teachings and doctrines are not accepted on blind faith in Buddhism, this does not mean that they are unimportant. The many Buddhist teachings work as maps would, to help you plan your spiritual journey. Another analogy often used is that the teachings offer you a boat that will carry you across a river. Daily chanting and meditation may sometimes seem a bit pointless, but when you practice them with sincerity, these things can have a profound impact on your outlook and life.

Even though many would tell you that Buddhism is not all about believing things, this doesn't mean that there are not Buddhist beliefs. In the centuries since its founding, Buddhism has sprouted diverse schools with doctrines that are distinctive and sometimes even contradictory. You may occasionally read or hear that "Buddhists believe" a certain thing, when that thing is actually a doctrine only belonging to one school, rather than to Buddhism as a whole.

To make the matter more confusing, there is also folk Buddhism in Asia. In this sect, Buddha and other Buddhist literature's iconic characters are believed to be truly divine beings who can listen to your prayers and grant you wishes. But if you focus on these beliefs, you really won't learn about Buddhism as a whole.

As a beginner learning about Buddhism, you should probably put aside any assumptions you may have. Also put aside religious assumptions and assumptions about existence, of the self and of reality. Open yourself to new understandings. The beliefs you do hold should be held in an open hand and with an open mind, rather than in a tight fist with a closed mind. Spend some time practicing and see where that will take you.

The Four Noble Truths

The First Noble Truth

This truth states that life includes suffering. Every life will see misery, aging, illness and finally death. These are all types of suffering. Although many people strive to find pleasure in life, they may receive pain instead. Despair, grief, pain, lamentation and sorrow are a part of life. Even if people achieve some happiness, they become tired of it and discontent once more.

The Second Noble Truth

This is the cause of people's suffering. Greed and desire will always lead to feelings of dissatisfaction. Attachment to and craving for sensual pleasures, ambition and desires to end sorrow are causes for rebirth, and this brings about more suffering.

The Third Noble Truth

This truth is the end of suffering. When you relinquish desires and craving, your discontentment and suffering will end, and you will feel peace and satisfaction.

The Fourth Noble Truth

This is the path to the ceasing of your suffering. Buddha taught his followers a Middle Way, which avoids excessive hardship AND excessive seeking of pleasure. This middle way will lead you to enlightenment, which is known as the Noble Eightfold Path.

The Noble Eightfold Path

The Eightfold Path starts at Right Understanding, which arises from the original first three Noble Truths, with seeing everything that is not permanent. Right Intention is developed from this awareness, and with it an aspiration to goodness, truth and beauty. These will lead to good personal conduct, which comes in the form of Right Livelihood, Right Speech and Right Action.

When you achieve these Right states, you will take responsibility for your own body, your speech and behavior. This means acting in ways that don't harm anyone else, in addition to following a strict moral code, and acting with compassion and non-violence. Finally, you will reach Right Concentration, Right Effort and Right Mindfulness. These are purposefully developed within your heart, through your meditation.

The Divine and Karma

In Buddhism, there is no belief in one god. In some Buddhist forms, there is no god at all. However, Mahayana Buddhism, in Korea, Japan, Mongolia, Tibet and China, teaches that there are many deities. It also elevates Buddha into the origin of everything that exists, and a divine being.

Buddhists believe in actions that are based on your desires, otherwise known as the power of Karma. Your actions, whether bad or good, make you continue in your cycle of reincarnation, which means that you are reborn over and over again until you finally achieve enlightenment.

The Five Buddhist Precepts

Buddha taught Five Precepts to help you in your everyday life.

- No harm to any living creature

- No taking more than you need

- No stealing and give generously

- No lying

- No acting thoughtlessly

Teachers of Buddhism draw on these important precepts in order to explain the importance of conserving.

These are some of the most basic beliefs of most Buddhists. Depending on the particular sects, there may be others, but these are the ones that most beginners will be learning if they wish to practice Buddhism.

CHAPTER 3 – How can Buddhism help you live a Balanced Life?

It wasn't long ago that the majority of Americans took their personal religion largely for granted. Most people stayed in the religion they were born into until they died. Except for freethinkers, that's how things were up until the 1950s. It's actually still the state of religion in most of our world.

Religion has not maintained that continuity in the United States. Today, many Americans don't identify themselves with any particular religion.

A recent poll by Pew Research reported that about 20% of adult Americans do not describe themselves as being affiliated with any religion. The percentage is even higher among younger adults, up to 72% for Generation Y.

People who become disenfranchised with their previous religion have many reasons. Most of them have a yearning for something much more than a life filled with materialism. They look for happiness and deeper meaning, and something they call "spiritual".

These reasons may be yours, too. You may be someone who is discovering all that Buddhism offers to your spiritual practice and life, without institutionalized religion's downsides.

May Buddhism be Right for you if you don't like Religion?

Among the major religions, Buddhism is unique. It's nontheistic and has no god. This changes a lot of things. Buddhism does describe a spiritual, non-material reality and does address what happens after you die.

However, it is also practical and down-to-earth. It is all about you, your mind and your suffering. Buddhism is about being deeply and fully human, and offers something to everyone.

How else is Buddhism Different?

The essence of Buddhism is meditation. It is contemplative and this reflects on its non-theism. It is about not divine authority or institutions, but about experience and realization. This makes the religion particularly well-suited to people who feel that they are not religious, but spiritual.

Here are some reasons why this is so:

Buddhism is about basic goodness.

Buddhism isn't about original sin or salvation. It isn't about going somewhere else or becoming someone different. It's about your world – and you – being basically good. With all its trials, our world works. You are warm, you are fed. You are offered sound, color and touch. The world is not against you, nor is it for you. So you don't have to struggle.

There is not a god in Buddhism.

Different Buddhism schools have differing views about who the actual Buddha was. Some feel that he was just a human being who discovered the path toward awakening. Others say that he was enlightened first, but followed that path in order to show people how it could be done.

One thing, however, is certain. Buddha was not a divine being, god or deity. His faculties were all human, so anyone can follow the path he took, and if you do, your enlightenment will be just the same as Buddha's was. Ultimately, Buddha was no different from you, nor you from him.

The problem humans face is suffering and the answer to that suffering is simply waking up.

Buddhism is in existence to address suffering. Buddha called suffering a noble truth because when you recognize your suffering, that is the inspiration and starting point of your spiritual path.

The second noble truth included the reasons for suffering. In the Western world, Buddhists refer to this as "ego". Although this is just a small word, it encompasses basically everything that is wrong with our world. That is due to the fact that Buddha tells us that all suffering, both small and large, starts with your false belief in a continuous, separate, solid "I", whose survival you devote your life to.

It probably feels like you are hopelessly caught up in a bad dream the world has created, of "you and them". You can awaken from that dream, though. This is the basis for the end of suffering, and the third noble truth.

You end suffering by recognizing your ignorance and the falsehood of your belief in the "I". Buddha tells you that to get to the end of suffering, using wisdom, meditation, effort and discipline. That is the truth of the path, which is the fourth noble truth.

You do this by working along with your own mind.

Buddha stated that while suffering is the problem, the actual cause is simple ignorance. The remedy is to wake up, and the path is to live mindfully, with meditation and the cultivation of your wisdom. This can only happen in your mind. The mind is the main source of suffering, but also of joy. Taming your mind through meditation is what will lead you from suffering into joy. Buddhism's special genius and remedy for the basic human condition is meditation.

No one else can do this for you, but you can do it.

There isn't a single savior in Buddhism. No one will do anything for you, and there are no places where you can hide from suffering. You must squarely face reality and you must do it yourself. Even when Buddhists decide to take refuge in the Buddha, they are not seeking protection, since there can be no protection from life.

The bad news, then, is the fact that you must ease suffering yourself, alone. But the good news is that you can truly do it. You have resources as a human being, including loving hearts, strength, intelligence and effective, proven methods. Because of those, you can rouse your confidence and thus renounce your resentment and depression.

Even though no one can do this for you, there is guidance and help available. Teachers, who are further along the right path, can offer you inspiration and instruction. They will prove to you that it can be done.

Your fellow Buddhists support your path, even though they will not allow you to use them for your crutches. Buddhist wisdom comes from 2,600 years ago, from the Buddha. You can go to that source, because the lineage that was started with the Buddha has not been broken, even up through today.

CHAPTER 4 – How to Appreciate Buddhism even if you're not Spiritual

Since Buddhism is essentially meditation, there are additional reasons why it is well-suited for people are feel more spiritual than religious:

Nothing must be taken on faith.

Buddhism has no received wisdom, or anything you have to accept just because someone else has, who has spiritual authority. The Dalai Lama states that if you follow Buddhism, you must give up beliefs that are disproven by modern science. The one Buddha even stated that you must be a lamp for yourself. This means testing everything against your personal experience.

Don't misinterpret that advice, though. Your modern ego wishes to take advantage of this. While you should not accept what people say simply at face value, that doesn't mean accepting what you tell yourself. You must test Buddhism's teachings against your own life experience, rather than against your opinions.

While modern science can disprove many older beliefs regarding human physiology or astronomy, it still can't test or measure things that are non-material. Studying Buddhism means valuing your rational mind, and seeking not to cause contradiction.

A person who can navigate a spiritual path without help is rare. While you retain your judgment and self-respect, you must be open to leadership and guidance from people further along the spiritual path. In our society, which exalts individuals and questions teacher-student relationships, it may be a challenge for you to find the middle ground between not enough self and too much.

There is a nonmaterial, spiritual reality.

While Buddhism has been described as scientific and rational, which helps you to lead a more caring and helpful life, this won't contradict your modern world view. Many practices of Buddhism work well in the modern world. They benefit people and don't require you to believe exotic things.

Buddhism does assert that beyond the material things in life is a more important reality. Other religions may say that, as well. The difference here is that the more important reality in Buddhism isn't a god. It is the mind.

Where is the boundary of your mind? Is it small or large? Is in within you and looking outside to our material world? Or are your experiences and perceptions found in both of these?

Buddhism is not institutional, but rather progressive and open.

Asian Buddhists may be more conservative, but those in the West who convert to Buddhism are largely liberal, both politically and socially. We don't know whether this is a natural reflection of the teachings of Buddha or an accident of history. Buddhist communities work against racism and sexism and embrace diversity.

The variety of identities in our world, like religion, ethnicity, nationality and gender are not seen in Buddhism as static. However, they are not denied, either. Differences are not only acknowledged, but enjoyed and even celebrated. Buddhists are still human and a part of our society, so it's rather like a work in progress, but they do try, unlike many people.

Buddhism offers you many skills for many needs of the people.

Buddhism is not a religion that offers one path that fits all situations. It's very much pragmatic, since it is centered on things that will reduce suffering. Buddhists do not seek to convert people, in the sense that many religions do. But there are people to help you if you freely choose this path.

As a being, you are infinite. So are your states of mind and problems. Buddhism offers you a wealth of knowledge and skill to meet the various needs that people have. If others are not ready to accept the final truth, but they can handle a partial truth, this is fine, as long as it helps them.

The issue sometimes arises when things that feel like they're helpful, like going along with life as usual, can make things worse, at times. Buddhist teachings can be tough, but are basically gentle. You must face the ways by which you cause suffering for yourself and others.

Meditators of Buddhism have studied the mind for thousands of years. They have tested and ultimately proven many helpful techniques that will lesson your suffering, tame your mind and allow you to discover who you are, what things are real, and which things are not.

You will find meditations that focus and calm the mind, meditations that will open your heart and methods for bringing grace and ease to your body. Many people say that Buddhism is the most developed science of mind in the world.

Today, the people who wish to explore Buddhism are blessed with many handy resources. All the traditions and schools of Buddhism are gathered together for the first time in human history. There are excellent teachers (including Americans), fine books, magazines, practice centers and communities. These are available to you if you wish to explore, according to your personal needs and the path you will choose.

You can meditate at home or practice the art with others at local centers. You may opt to attend classes, read books, study online or hear lectures from Buddhist teachers. Choose the method that works the best for you, with no pressure.

Buddhism works.

You cannot measure or even see subjective experience. Thus, you cannot judge the direct effect that Buddhism has on a person's heart and mind. But you can see the way they act, and the way they treat others. You can hear what they say about the things they experience deep inside.

What has been found is simply that Buddhism works for many people. It has been making people more skillful, aware and caring, for millennia. If you meet someone who practices meditating a lot, you'll see that.

In our current times, with much confusion and hardship in the world, hundreds of thousands of everyday Americans have reported that even modest practice of Buddhism helped to calm them and make them feel happier. They don't get as carried away with strong emotions, when they arise. They are kinder to others – and to themselves.

This in no way is an attempt to convert you to Buddhism. They have no need to convert people, and it isn't a part of their philosophy. But if you feel that you are spiritual without being religious, you may find a great deal of help on your own personal path through Buddhism, however you may define that path.

When you encounter Buddhism for the first time, you may be struck by its integrity. It will not manipulate you by telling you what you want to hear. It tells the truth, always. Sometimes you will find the truth to be gentle, which could bring tears to your eyes and soften your heart. But sometimes the truth is tough, and this forces you to face your problems and cut through your illusions. The truth of Buddhism is always skillful, though. It will always offer you what you need, and you are free to take whatever you need to find the path to ease your suffering.

CHAPTER 5 – Living Life in the Buddhist Faith

If you already know the reasons people have when they convert to Christianity, you may wonder why Buddhists on the spiritual path do not have the conversion reasons. Quite simply, they don't need them. They are always there, but no one seems to need a list. If it's right for you, then you'll know it.

Buddhism isn't right for everyone. It requires much dedication and discipline, and the doctrines are sometimes difficult to wrap your head around. In addition, people who are not Buddhists may see you as a flower child of some sort.

Most people don't convert directly into Buddhism. They have the religion of their birth (if their family practiced a religion) and there is usually a period of not being affiliated with any religion before you move toward Buddhism.

Searching for Transcendence

One false assumption of any religion is believing that one must believe the "correct" beliefs and think the "correct" thoughts in order to define a religion. Religion is not just about beliefs. It's actually a search for transcendence.

You can conceptualize transcendence in many ways, of course. You might think of it as entry into Nirvana or uniting with God. Yet conceptualizations are not as important as you might think, since they are all imperfect. Is Nirvana a metaphor for God? Is God a metaphor for Nirvana?

Buddha taught the original monks that they could not conceptualize Nirvana. God refused to be represented in an image or limited by a name in Exodus. It is sometimes hard for us to accept, but there will always be places where your intellect and imagination can't go.

A True Religion

People seeking to convert others into their chosen religion usually believe that their religion is the only "right" one. They believe that only their doctrines are true and that their God is the only God, and everyone else is wrong. Thinking like this makes an assumption that is rejected by many Buddhists.

The main assumption that we, with only human intellect, could ever understand an omnipotent God, is the mistake. Not only is that impossible, but how can you express it to others with full accuracy?

Most Buddhists feel that no religion, including their own, holds complete truth. Every religion falls short of full understanding. They are all misunderstood frequently. Even the truest doctrines may be perceived as merely shadows on the wall or pointers.

It could be that most religious doctrines reflect one small part of an absolute and great truth, so their beliefs aren't false, either. All religions are true in their own way. You just need to try to understand to what degree they are true.

Lights in the Darkness

Doctrines and beliefs have value, regardless of the religion you practice. Doctrines can help you like a candle when you're walking in darkness. They can work as markers do on a path, which show you the way that others before you have walked.

In Buddhism, the value of doctrines is judged not on facts but by its skillfulness. Each skillful doctrine will open your mind to wisdom and your heart to compassion.

Beliefs that are rigidly fixed, however, are not skillful. They seal you off from objective reality, and from people who do not share your beliefs. They harden your mind and close you to other realizations and revelations that Grace could send your way.

One True Religion

All of the world's greatest religions arguably accumulate their share of practices and doctrines, both unskillful and skillful. However, even when a religion works well for one person, it may not work well for another. The one true religion that works for you will ultimately be the one that engages most completely your mind and heart. This type of engagement enables transcendence.

Some people who are Buddhists now left Christianity because it didn't engage their minds and hearts anymore. That doesn't mean that Christianity is wrong for everyone. Nor is any other religion wrong for everyone.

This author spoke last week to someone who attends a synagogue. It was clear from his speaking that he was passionate about Judaism, and that it filled his life. It was indeed his one true religion. Buddhism does not teach its members to try to convert people from religions that already work for them.

Engaged Buddhism

The first precept from Buddhist Thich Nhat Hanh is that you should not be bound to or idolatrous about a doctrine, ideology or theology, even those that are Buddhist. The systems of thought in Buddhism are a means of guidance, not an absolute truth.

This is why many people enter Buddhism. It is a religion that allows you to feel its light with your entire mind and heart, without discarding your critical thinking skills. This is also one of the reasons why Buddhists do not seek to convert people from other religions.

If you seek a spiritual home, you will find many people that will help you, as a beginner to Buddhism. But they will not try to convert you. The reasons you choose Buddhism will be found in your own heart.

CONCLUSION

Since we are all human, we share a desire for meaning and happiness in our lives. Dalai Lama states that within everyone is the ability to find true fulfillment. We hope this e-book has helped you to embark on a life path to your enlightenment, with the timeless wisdom of Buddhism.

We have given you valuable information so that you can start a journey of wisdom, morality and meditation as a beginner to Buddhism. This book will help you to refrain from doing harm and to maintain your mental tranquility.

You will also learn the methods involved in overcoming everyday life obstacles, like counterproductive thinking, insecurity, jealousy and anger. When you become imbued with the vivacious spirit of Buddha, you will be empowered to lead a balanced life and learn a true spiritual path toward a brighter future.

19090482R00030

Printed in Great Britain
by Amazon